by Michael Sellers
illustrated by Catherine Lucas

HOUGHTON MIFFLIN   BOSTON

Printed in China

ISBN 10: 0-618-88688-5
ISBN 13: 978-0-618-88688-3

16 17 18 19 20 0940 21 20 19 18 17
4500648152

Marcie, Angela, and Rico collected comic books.

Mom said, "There are just too many comic books. At least 30 comic books must go."

Read • Think • Write Are there more than 30 comic books in the room?

2

The children took more than 30 comic books outside. They put them on a table. A boy came along. "Wow!" he said, "I'll buy 12."

Read • Think • Write How many comic books were on the table in all?

Marcie gave the boy 12 comic books. It wasn't very long until a girl came along. "I love comic books," she said. "I'll buy 9."

Read • Think • Write   How many comic books did the children have after they gave the boy 12 comic books?

Rico gave the girl 9 comic books. Right away, a woman came. "Oh, my children will like these," she said. "I will buy 10 comic books."

Read • Think • Write How many comic books did the children have after they gave the girl 9 comic books?

Angela gave the woman 10 comic books. In the blink of an eye, a boy came and said, "I'd like 6 comic books, please."

Read • Think • Write How many comic books did the children have after they gave the woman 10 comic books?

"We sold so many comic books,"said Rico.

"And we earned a penny for each one," said Angela.

"And we still have one comic book for each of us," said Marcie. "What a great day."

Read•Think•Write How many comic books did the children have in the end?

Comic Books for Sale

Show

Monitor/Clarify Look at page 4. Draw a picture to show how many comic books there were after Marcie gave the boy 12 comic books.

Share

Talk about the picture on page 4. Tell how the comic books are arranged.

Write

Look at page 4. Write how many comic books there are.